Characteristics of Spirit-led Prayer

The Bible Teacher's Guide

Gregory Brown

BTG
Publishing

4

Endorsements

"Expositional, theological, and candidly practical! I highly recommend *The Bible Teacher's Guide* for anyone seeking to better understand or teach God's Word."

—Dr. Young–Gil Kim, Founding President of Handong Global University

"Helpful to both the laymen and the serious student, *The Bible Teacher's Guide,* by Dr. Greg Brown, is outstanding!"

—Dr. Neal Weaver, President of Louisiana Baptist University

"Whether you are preparing a Bible study, a sermon, or simply wanting to dive deeper into a personal study of God's Word, these will be very helpful tools."

—Eddie Byun, Author of *Justice Awakening*

"I am happy that Greg is making his insights into God's truth available to a wider audience through these books. They bear the hallmarks of good Bible teaching: the result of rigorous Bible study and thoroughgoing application to the lives of people."

—Ajith Fernando, Teaching Director, Youth for Christ; Author of *A Call to Joy and Pain*

"The content of the series is rich. My prayer is that God will use it to help the body of Christ grow strong."

—Dr. Min Chung, Senior Pastor of Covenant Fellowship Church (Urbana, Illinois)

"*The Bible Teacher's Guide* is thorough but concise, with thought-provoking discussion questions in each section. This is a great tool for teaching God's Word."

—Dr. Steve Pettey, Dean of Louisiana Baptist Theological Seminary

"Knowing the right questions to ask and how to go about answering them is fundamental to learning in any subject matter. Greg demonstrates this convincingly."

—Dr. William Moulder, Professor of Biblical Studies at Trinity International University

"Pastor Greg is passionate about the Word of God, rigorous and thorough in his approach to the study of it... I am pleased to recommend *The Bible Teacher's*

Guide to anyone who hungers for the living Word."

—Dr. JunMo Cho, Worship Leader and Recording Artist; Professor of Linguistics at Handong Global University

"I can't imagine any student of Scripture not benefiting by this work."

—Steven J. Cole, Pastor, Flagstaff Christian Fellowship, Author of the *Riches from the Word* series

Contents

Preface

And the things you have heard me say in the
presence of many witnesses entrust to reliable
men who will also be qualified to teach others.
2 Timothy 2:2

Paul's words to Timothy still apply to us today. We
need to raise up teachers who correctly handle and
fearlessly teach the Word of God. It is with this hope in
mind that the Bible Teacher's Guide (BTG) series has
been created. The BTG series includes both
expositional studies and topical studies. This guide will
be useful for personal devotions, small groups, and for
teachers preparing to share God's Word.

Characteristics of Spirit-led Prayer is an excerpt and an
adaptation from the larger work BTG Colossians. It can
be used as a two to six-week small-group curriculum
depending on how the leader chooses to divide the
introduction and the five characteristics. Every week,
the members of the group will read a chapter or more,
answer the questions, and come prepared to share in the
gathering. Each member's preparation for the small
group will enrich the discussion and the learning.

Introduction

"For this reason, since the day we heard about you, we have not stopped praying for you and asking God to fill you with the knowledge of his will through all spiritual wisdom and understanding. And we pray this in order that you may live a life worthy of the Lord and may please him in every way: bearing fruit in every good work, growing in the knowledge of God, being strengthened with all power according to his glorious might so that you may have great endurance and patience, and joyfully giving thanks to the Father, who has qualified you to share in the inheritance of the saints in the kingdom of light. For he has rescued us from the dominion of darkness and brought us into the kingdom of the Son he loves, in whom we have redemption, the forgiveness of sins" (Col. 1:9–14).

Do you ever struggle with how to pray? Do you ever struggle with what words to say or knowing if you're praying exactly what God's will is?

In this text, we see Paul praying God's will for the church. We can be sure that it's God's will and Spirit–led because God chose to include this prayer in the Holy Scripture as an example for us.

Paul had never seen or met with this church before (cf. Col. 2:1). At the time of this writing, Paul is in prison, and it was one of his disciples, Epaphras, who previously founded this church.

Shortly after Epaphras founded the church of Colosse, a group of false teachers entered the church and caused division. From the clues in the letter, it seems that this group was influenced by Gnostic teaching. The word *gnostic* comes from the Greek word *gnosko*, "to know." They said in order for a person to be saved or in order for them to be sanctified, they had to experience supernatural knowledge. They needed new revelation.

This is very much like many of the cults and liberal Christian groups today. They teach that the revelation of Scripture is not enough. They say the Bible is either not true or we need human reason to test the writings of Scripture to see what is true. They declare the revelation of Scripture is not enough and that there is a new authoritative revelation that all must hear.

This Gnostic teaching, just like Satan in the Garden, attacked the very foundation of our faith, which is the Word of God. Because the Colossian church was experiencing this teaching, it was in great trouble. The ground of their faith had been shaken as Satan, through false teaching, attacked the gospel message and Christ specifically.

But as we look at this prayer, we learn a lot about how we should pray for God's church, which is always being attacked from without and within. This prayer shows us how we can intercede for the body of Christ throughout the world, for believers we know and those we don't know. The characteristics of prayer in this text will strengthen our own prayer life. Let's look at the text and see what we can learn.

Reflection

1. How would you describe your prayer life? What are its strengths and weakness?
2. What are some disciplines that help your prayer life?
3. What are some things that distract your prayer life?
4. What other questions or thoughts do you have about this section?
5. In what ways can you pray in response? Take a second to pray as the Lord leads.

Spirit–led Prayer Is Informed

"For this reason, since the day *we heard about you* we have not stopped praying for you" (Col. 1:9).

Paul says, *"For this reason, since the day we heard about you, we have not stopped praying for you."* Paul was not just sitting in his room, and the Holy Spirit brought the exact prayer prompts to his mind without outside information. No, his prayer was informed.

It seems that Epaphras had informed Paul about the needs of the church and the attack of the cult. It was this information that led Paul into deep prayer. Part of the reason many of us struggle with our prayer life is because we are not informed. We don't know how to pray or what to pray for.

We don't know the problems of our friends, our church, our company, or our nation. Some of us do not want to know what everybody else struggles with. Listen to what Solomon said: "The heart of the wise is in the house of mourning, but the heart of fools is in the house of pleasure" (Eccl. 7:4).

"The heart of the wise is in the house of mourning." The wise want to be where there is hurting and pain, but the fool wants nothing to do with it. The fool thinks his happiness and pleasure is all that matters in life, so he goes off seeking solely those things. For the fool, "Ignorance is truly bliss."

But this is not true for the wise. They know "joy" can be found even in the midst of suffering. The wise know this and choose to be informed, even if that means being at the hospital with someone sick or dying, or inquiring and asking questions about issues and problems in the church. That's what the wise will do. The wise are not living for themselves but to serve God and others.

We get a glimpse of this in the example of Nehemiah. Let's look at the beginning of his story.

> The words of Nehemiah son of Hacaliah: In the month of Kislev in the twentieth year, while I was in the citadel of Susa, Hanani, one of my brothers, came from Judah with some other men, and I questioned them about the Jewish remnant that survived the exile, and also about Jerusalem. They said to me, 'Those who survived the exile and are back in the province are in great trouble and disgrace. The wall of Jerusalem is broken down, and its gates have been burned with fire.' When I heard these things, I sat down and wept. For some days I mourned and fasted and prayed before the God of heaven (Neh. 1:1–4).

Nehemiah was the cupbearer of the king of Persia. He had no worries and no needs. He lived in the palace. However, this was no excuse for him to be blind to the pains of the world and especially to those of the people of God. When his brother visited the kingdom, he asked him about the Jews left in Israel and about the city of Jerusalem.

Upon hearing the seriousness of the situation, he went into deep fasting and mourning. He took on their pain and wept for them, and then he felt compelled to return to Israel and help. Nehemiah was informed and that prompted his prayer life, and therefore, his mission.

We must be informed as well. I think Paul is telling us to be informed in Colossians 4:2 when he says to be "watchful" so we can pray. "Devote yourselves to prayer, being watchful and thankful."

We must be watchful so we can be informed and know how to pray. *How do we become informed so that we can pray properly?*

1. To be informed we must be sensitive to the needs of others.

Sometimes people may choose not to share what is wrong or burdening them and the intercessor is left to his discernment. This is not as difficult as it sounds. Communication is over 70 percent nonverbal. Many times you can tell something is wrong with a person by what their body is saying or by what their mouth is not saying.

A person who is sensitive, who desires to know the needs and concerns of others, many times identifies cues others miss. We need to look at our friend's body language, our wife's body language, and discern what they might not be saying.

In fact, we see this with King Artaxerxes and Nehemiah in Chapter 2. Look at the story:

In the month of Nisan in the twentieth year of King Artaxerxes, when wine was brought for him, *I took the wine and gave it to the king. I had not been sad in his presence before; so the king asked me, 'Why does your face look so sad when you are not ill? This* can be nothing but sadness of heart.' I was very much afraid (Neh. 2:1–2).

See, the king picked up on the sadness in Nehemiah's heart, which prompted him to ask a question. We must be sensitive and discerning as well. This leads us to the second way we can be informed.

2. To be informed we must be willing to ask the right questions.

What are the right questions? It is not, "What do you think about the weather?" or "How about those Chicago Bulls?" It means asking questions that tell us something about their heart and their relationship with God.

Nehemiah asked his brother about how things were going with the remnant of Israel, and this prompted him to prayer. Asking the right questions may include things like:

- How is your relationship with God?
- Have you been reading the Word of God?
- How are you and your boyfriend doing with staying pure?
- How are you handling temptation on the Internet?

We must learn to ask the right questions. This is essentially one of the greatest skills a counselor must develop to help people. This is also true for someone who is an intercessor. The right question can be as simple as, "How can I be praying for you at this time?"

3. To be informed we must be aware of what is happening in society and the world.

When Nehemiah asked his brother about Israel, this was a world event—world news. The news was about the Jews who returned after the Babylonian exile.

In the same way, one of the ways we can be informed is by something as simple as watching the news or reading news online. We should do this not just to accumulate knowledge but also to be drawn to prayer.

If we hear about difficulties in Egypt, Syria, Iraq, or North Korea, then it should prompt us to prayer. Prayer is not getting our will done on earth, but God's will done. God cares about the nations, the people who are hungry, suffering, and at war. Informed Christians should be drawn to prayer over world events.

4. To be informed we must be sensitive to the promptings of the Spirit of God.

Sometimes the Spirit of God prompts us to pray specifically for a situation or a person. We see this in Acts 13. The disciples fasted and prayed in Antioch, and the Spirit of the Lord told them to set apart Barnabas and Paul for the mission work he had called them to. Acts 13:1–3 says this:

> In the church at Antioch there were prophets and teachers: Barnabas, Simeon called Niger, Lucius of Cyrene, Manaen (who had been

brought up with Herod the tetrarch) and Saul. *While they were worshiping the Lord and fasting, the Holy Spirit said, 'Set apart for me Barnabas and Saul for the work to which I have called them.'* So after they had fasted and prayed, they placed their hands on them and sent them off.

After this prompting, the leaders of the Antioch church laid hands on Paul and Barnabas and sent them out to do missions in the Gentile world. In some sense, we are here as Gentiles because of that mission and because they were sensitive to the Holy Spirit.

In the same way, we should be sensitive to the Holy Spirit in our prayers. I often practice asking the Holy Spirit how he would have me pray. I do this especially when I'm struggling with what to say or pray about. Scripture says one of the Holy Spirit's jobs is to help us with our prayers. Romans 8:26 says, "In the same way, the Spirit helps us in our weakness. We do not know what we ought to pray for, but *the Spirit himself intercedes for us with groans that words cannot express.*"

How else can we be informed like Paul so that we can pray?

5. To be informed we must know the Word of God.

The Word of God often clearly tells us how God wants Christians to pray. For instance 1 Timothy 2:1–3 says this:

I urge, then, first of all, that requests, prayers, intercession and thanksgiving be made for everyone—for kings and all those in authority, that we may live peaceful and quiet lives in all godliness and holiness. This is good, and pleases God our Savior.

When we pray for our pastors, teachers, government leaders, presidents, etc., we can be sure we are praying as the Spirit desires. This is exactly what Scripture calls Christians to pray for. We pray for these things especially in the places where we live so we can live peaceful and godly lives. These types of prayers help keep our government from corruption, ungodly laws, and decrees.

We also see *commands to pray for all Christians—the entire church—in Scripture.* Look at what Paul says in Ephesians 6:18: "And pray in the Spirit on all occasions with all kinds of prayers and requests. With this in mind, be alert and *always keep on praying for all the saints.*"

When we lift up local churches and the universal church throughout the world, we can be sure we are being directed by the Spirit. Often, Christians have a tendency to think only of their local church and forget that the body of Christ is larger than their congregation or local association. Informed prayer includes things that God has called us to pray for in Scripture.

To be Spirit–led in prayer we must be informed just as Paul received updates from Epaphras. Let us seek to be informed Christians so we can be Spirit–led intercessors.

1. In what ways do you practice being informed in your prayer life?
2. How is God calling you to be more strategic in being informed?
3. What other questions or thoughts do you have about this section?
4. In what ways can you pray in response? Take a second to pray as the Lord leads.

Spirit–led Prayer Is Constant

"For this reason, since the day we heard about you, *we have not stopped praying for you*" (Col. 1:9).

Another characteristic of Spirit–led prayer is that it is constant or without ceasing. Paul says, "We have not stopped praying for you." After Epaphras informed Paul about the situation in Colosse, he did not simply pray once and forget the topic. He faithfully continued to pray for this church. This is something that Scripture commands of us. Listen to what Paul says in 1 Thessalonians 5:16–17: "Be joyful always; pray continually."

How do we practice a lifestyle of praying without ceasing?

1. To pray without ceasing, we must develop a God–consciousness.

John MacArthur has tremendous insights on how to do this practically. Look what he said:

Such unceasing or recurring prayer (1 Thess. 5:17) demands first of all an *attitude of God–consciousness*. That does not mean to be constantly in the act of verbal prayer, but to

25

view everything in life in relation to God. For example, if we meet someone, we immediately consider where they stand with God. If we hear of something bad happening, we react by praying for God to act in the situation because we know He cares. If we hear of something good that has happened, we respond with immediate praise to God for it because we know He is glorified. When Paul looked around his world, everything he saw prompted him to prayer in some way. When he thought of or heard about one of his beloved churches, it moved him toward communion with God.[i]

If we are going to develop constancy in prayer, we also must develop a God–consciousness where we view every person and situation from the standpoint of God. Listen to what Paul said: "So from now on we regard no one from a worldly point of view. Though we once regarded Christ in this way, we do so no longer" (2 Cor. 5:16).

Paul could not look at people the way he once did. We look at people as "Dr. So-and-so" or "the wife of James," but Paul always viewed them as souls for whom Christ died. He saw them in relation to God and his plan for their lives. Therefore, he was always moved to prayer.

The secular viewpoint regards the world without God, and therefore sees no need for him or prayer. But to view life from God's view is to see the weakness and corruption of man and the world system and its need for God. This prompted Paul to live in prayer, and it should do the same to us.

It should be noted that being God–conscious makes a person automatically *self–conscious and others-conscious.* We see this with Isaiah when he saw God in heaven in Isaiah 6:5. Listen to what he said: "'Woe to me!' I cried. 'I am ruined! For I am a man of unclean lips, and I live among a people of unclean lips, and my eyes have seen the King, the LORD Almighty.'"

Isaiah saw God and it automatically affected how he saw himself and others. It prompted him to prayer. He began to lament before God because of his sinful state and that of his people.

Similarly, when one lives in a state of consciousness toward God, he will find that watching the news or other events may be a very difficult chore. He will find himself at times prompted to lament and lift up individuals, the church, and society. This is a good thing.

We must develop this type of mindset to pray without ceasing as Paul did.

Application Question: What are some other biblical or practical examples of implementing this lifestyle of constant prayer?

Nehemiah is a good example of someone who lived in prayer. In his book, we see him pray eleven times. One great example of this is in Nehemiah 2:4–5. Nehemiah has just told the king about the desperate circumstances of his nation, and then the king said, "What is it you want?" Look at how Scripture describes his reply: "Then I prayed to the God of heaven, and I answered the king" (Neh. 2:5).

It says he prayed to the God of heaven and then answered the king. Now did Nehemiah stop and get on his knees, talk to God, and then reply to the king? Probably not. Often people call this an *arrow prayer*. He was talking to the king and while doing this he shot up a prayer to God. See, Nehemiah was God–conscious even while talking to the king. He knew his weakness and he probably feared for his life. To be sad in front of the king could actually call for his execution. In view of this, he prays to the God of heaven while having a conversation.

We can do this throughout the day as well. We don't need to walk around with our hands folded while praying. We can lift up prayers to the God of heaven throughout the day. Listen to this other practical illustration of praying constantly about a woman named Aunt Vertie.

> Aunt Vertie, one of the godliest women I have ever heard about, was once asked the meaning of 'praying without ceasing.' She replied: 'Well, it means what it says:
> "When I put on my clothes in the morning, I thank God for clothing me in the righteousness of Christ.
> When I wash in the morning, I ask God to cleanse me from my sin.
> When I eat breakfast, I thank Christ for being the bread of life.
> When I clean house, I ask God to be merciful and cleanse the houses of the world from sin.
> When I talk with people throughout the day, I ask God to save and grow them in Christ and to meet their particular needs.

When I see strangers or crowds of people on the streets, I pray for the salvation of the people of the world.""[ii]

Amen! We can live a lifestyle of constant prayer as we see God in everything. We can see him in our eating, drinking, and our studying, and this can prompt us to constant prayer. This is the desire of the Spirit of God in our lives.

Reflection

1. What are some other tips to help us be more constant in prayer like Paul?
2. What tactics do you use?
3. What other questions or thoughts do you have about this section?
4. In what ways can you pray in response? Take a second to pray as the Lord leads.

Spirit–led Prayer Asks for God–sized Requests

Another thing we must notice about Paul's prayers is that they were God–sized. His requests were not stingy. Consider some of the superlatives he used:

> For this reason, since the day we heard about you, we have not stopped praying for you and asking God to fill you with the knowledge of his will through *all spiritual wisdom* and understanding. And we pray this in order that you may live a life worthy of the Lord and may *please him in every way*: *bearing fruit in every good work*, growing in the knowledge of God, being *strengthened with all power* according to his glorious might so that you *may have great endurance and patience* (Col. 1:9–11).

Do you see all the superlatives Paul uses? He asks for "all spiritual wisdom and understanding" to "please him in every way, bearing fruit in every good work" to be "strengthened with all power" for them to "have great endurance and patience."

When you listen to most people's prayers, you would think they are talking to a very small God. But, when the Spirit of God is guiding our prayers, he knows and calls upon the tremendous resources that we have access to in God.

A perfect example of this is *Christ*. Scripture shows us the type of prayers he prayed. Look at what God commands him to pray in Psalm 2:8, a messianic Psalm. It says, "Ask of me, and I will make the nations your inheritance, the ends of the earth your possession."

Again, we see that God is calling him to pray a big prayer. The Holy Spirit is prompting him to ask for the nations. Similarly, God often calls us to pray big prayers in order to bring glory to him.

Certainly, we see this when we look at *Moses* in Exodus 33:18. It says, "Then Moses said, 'Now show me your glory.'" Moses's request was so grand God had to dial it down a bit. He declared to Moses, in the preceding verses, he could not show his face, but that Moses would see the glory of his arms and back. Spirit–led prayers ask for God–sized requests.

We have seen this in the history of the church by those whom God has used greatly. *John Knox*, a man used greatly for Christ in Scotland, prayed this prayer: "Give me Scotland or I die." Mary the Queen of the Scotts said that she was more afraid of John Knox's prayers than an army of ten thousand.

George Whitefield, an evangelist in the 18th-century who was used to start a revival in England that later spilled over into America, once prayed: "Lord give me souls or take my soul." It was said that when he preached, hundreds of people would fall down under the conviction of sin.

Both of these men were used greatly by God. We also see this in the story of *Dawson Trotman*, founder of the Navigators. The Navigators is a ministry that is happening all over the world, and it was started by a man who was willing to ask God for great things. Let's look at this small selection from an article written about him:

> The Word of God was foremost in his thinking, and he saturated himself with it . . . memorizing a verse a day, studying it, reading it, praying over it. He found promises like Jeremiah 33:3 and Ephesians 3:20 and wondered at their depthless possibilities. 'Call unto Me, and I will answer thee, and show thee great and mighty things, which thou knowest not.' 'Now unto Him that is able to do exceeding abundantly above all that we ask or think, according to the power that worketh in us . . . '

> If these were God's promises, they were meant to be claimed. Dawson asked a friend if he would join him in asking God for some of these great things. The friend agreed, and following the example of the Lord Jesus in rising early, they met in the hills at five o'clock every morning of the week. They prayed until seven, and were at work by the scheduled eight o'clock. Dawson as a truck driver and the other man as a plumber.

> The two determined to continue until they were sure God would show them some of the great and mighty things He had promised. They prayed at first for the boys in the Bible clubs by name and for the towns nearby from which requests had come for help with their boys. Then they prayed for cities up and down the

California coast. As they prayed, God enlarged their vision, and they began to ask that God would use them and other young fellows in each of the 48 States.

During the sixth week God put it into their hearts to pray for the world. With a map before them they put their fingers on Okinawa, Formosa, Germany, France, Turkey, Greece . . . praying that God would use them in the lives of men in those places. After 42 days the burden lifted. There was nothing left to ask, and they knew their purpose had been accomplished. [iii]

Dawson had a burden that led to forty-two days of praying. The fruit of this praying is a ministry that is affecting people all over the world. It started by praying for great things.

Is this not why James encourages us to pray for the healing of the sick? He says the prayers of a righteous man are powerful. Consider what he says:

Therefore confess your sins to each other and pray for each other so that you may be healed. *The prayer of a righteous man is powerful and effective.* Elijah was a man just like us. He prayed earnestly that it would not rain, and it did not rain on the land for three and a half years. Again he prayed, and the heavens gave rain, and the earth produced its crops (James 5:16–18).

In what ways is the Spirit of God calling you to pray big prayers?

I'll be honest. Even as I talk about this, I have a fear praying these types of prayers. Do I really want to be used by God in a great way? Also, am I selfless enough to be willing to pray for others' ministries that God would use them greatly? Am I willing to pray that he would give them all knowledge, all power? These are great things to pray for, and I believe that is how the Holy Spirit desires us to pray.

Listen to how Paul ends his prayers for the Ephesians. He says:

> Now to him *who is able to do immeasurably more than all we ask or imagine, according to his power that is at work within us*, to him be glory in the church and in Christ Jesus throughout all generations, for ever and ever! Amen (Eph. 3:20–21).

God is able. Let Paul's prayers encourage us to pray for the members of our church to be strengthened with all power, to be filled with all the knowledge of God's will. Let this prayer encourage us to pray greatly for churches throughout the world that God would open doors to reach the youth, to be strategic in breaking trafficking and ministering to orphans, to reach a nation with the gospel, or to bring revival in their own nation. Let us pray for open doors for ministers in the church to love and care for the lost.

Let us even consider praying scary prayers for ourselves. Pray that God would use us greatly. Let us pray like Moses that we would see his glory. Let us pray like Paul in Ephesians 3:19, that we may be filled with the "fullness of God." Let our prayers demonstrate how great God is.

Reflection

1. In what ways is God stretching your faith and prayer life by calling you to pray God–sized prayers?
2. What are some hindrances to praying these types of prayers?
3. What other questions or thoughts do you have about this section?
4. In what ways can you pray in response? Take a second to pray as the Lord leads.

Spirit–led Prayer Is Consumed with God's Will

"Asking God to fill you with the knowledge of his will through all spiritual wisdom and understanding" (Col. 1:9b).

Here we see the content of Spirit–led prayer. Spirit–led prayer is always asking for God's will to be done. When Paul prays for believers to be filled with the knowledge of God's will, it essentially means two things:

(1) to know God's will and
(2) to do God's will.

The word "filled" has to do with being controlled. Paul is not just asking for head knowledge, but an intimate knowledge that controls the believer's life. We see this in how Ephesians 5:18–19 talks about being "filled" with the Spirit. Look at what it says:

> Do not get drunk on wine, which leads to debauchery. *Instead, be filled with the Spirit.* Speak to one another with psalms, hymns and spiritual songs. Sing and make music in your heart to the Lord.

To be filled with the Spirit means to be controlled by the Spirit in the same way someone drunk is controlled by wine. It means to submit to the will of the Spirit of God in our lives. Similarly, Paul prays this for the Colossians. He prays for this church to know God's will, probably specifically in confronting the heresy attacking the church. But, he also prays that this church be controlled by God's will as they obey it.

Most Prayer Is the Opposite

Now it should be mentioned that much of Christian prayer is not Spirit–led. Much of Christian prayer is often about getting our will done on earth. When Christ prayed, he prayed, "Lord, not my will but your will be done" (Luke 22:42). In fact, it is through prayer that many times our wills are conformed to God's will. This means that in the midst of prayer, we often start to be able to accept a trial we are going through, a difficult person we continually have conflict with, or any other event that has come our way. Prayer, ultimately, is to get God's will done on the earth as seen in the Lord's Prayer. "This, then, is how you should pray: 'Our Father in heaven, hallowed be your name, your kingdom come, your will be done on earth as it is in heaven'" (Matt. 6:9–10).

When Paul talks about being filled "*through all wisdom and understanding*," wisdom is simply the application of knowledge. It means to know what God's Word says and how to apply it. Understanding may mean how to apply this wisdom in various and different circumstances, maybe as we counsel others or make decisions about life.

38

Paul prays that the church would know God's will and have wisdom to apply it, and to have the understanding on when and where to appropriate it in different circumstances.

Warnings about Not Knowing

The knowledge of God's will is very important in the life of a believer. Scripture warns against not having this knowledge. Hosea 4:6 says this:

> *My people are destroyed from lack of knowledge.* 'Because you have rejected knowledge, I also reject you as my priests; because you have ignored the law of your God, I also will ignore your children.'

Hosea said the nation of Israel was rejected for a lack of knowledge. Similarly, Isaiah said they were kicked out of Canaan for a lack of knowledge of God. Listen to what he says: "Therefore my people will go into exile for lack of understanding; their men of rank will die of hunger and their masses will be parched with thirst" (Isa. 5:13).

In the same way, many Christians miss God's best because of this. They miss God's grace on their lives and find themselves in bondage to sin, in bondage to an addictive relationship, and in bondage to the world and its things because of a lack of knowledge.

The primary way we know the knowledge of the will of God is through his Word. A large aspect of our prayers should be for people to know the Word of God and have wisdom and understanding on how to apply it. Jesus prayed this similarly in John 17:17 as he prayed for all the church. He said, "Sanctify them by your truth, your word is truth."

Essentially, he prayed, "Make them holy through the Word of God." We should pray this as well, and we certainly should live it.

The great prayer of the church should be for people to know the will of God and for the government and our leaders to know the will of God. For lack of knowledge our churches perish, and for lack of knowledge our government comes under the judgment of God. We must pray not only that people would know God's will, but also that they would be filled and controlled by God's will. This is the content of Spirit–led prayer. "Your kingdom come, your will be done on earth as it is in heaven."

How can we be filled with the knowledge of God's will, both to know it and do it?

1. In order to be filled with the knowledge of God's will, we must first desire God's Word.

Everything starts with the right desire. The reason most Christians are not filled with the knowledge of God's will is not for a lack of access to it. We have the Bible; we have Bible-preaching churches; we have access to much spiritual food through the Internet. The major problem with Christians is not access. It is desire. Listen to how the Psalmist talks about the blessings on a man who delights in the Word of God.

> *But his delight is in the law of the LORD, and on his law he meditates day and night.* He is like

a tree planted by streams of water, which yields its fruit in season and whose leaf does not wither. Whatever he does prospers (Ps. 1:2–3).

David says God blesses the man who delights in the law of the LORD. This delight draws them to the Scripture all day long. We all know what it means to "delight" in something. It's like students on campus all day long looking at their smartphones, liking every comment that comes up on Facebook. Whatever you delight in, you will do all the time.

Peter says something similar: "Like newborn babies, crave pure spiritual milk, so that by it you may grow up in your salvation" (1 Peter 2:2).

This inner desire is so important Peter commands it. "Crave pure spiritual milk"; crave it like a newborn baby does. A newborn essentially eats all day long, and that's the type of desire a Christian should develop in his life for God's will—his Word.

What should a person do if they don't desire the Word of God?

A wise man once said, "Make it your discipline until it becomes your delight." Make it the first thing you do in the morning. Make it your snack throughout the day. Make it the last thing you do before bed. Cultivate a desire for the Word of God; cultivate a desire to always be seeking God's will.

Paul prayed for them to be filled with the knowledge of God's will and that starts off with having a healthy desire.

2. In order to be filled with God's will, we must depend on the Lord.

Scripture teaches that man in his natural state has a faculty problem. He cannot understand the things of God and they are foolishness to him if the Holy Spirit doesn't enable him. First Corinthians 2:14 says, "The man without the Spirit does not accept the things that come from the Spirit of God, for they are foolishness to him, and he cannot understand them, because they are spiritually discerned."

The unregenerate man reads the Bible and gets nothing from it. He cannot understand it, since he does not have the Holy Spirit. However, we do have the Holy Spirit, as he indwells every true believer. But, this does not change our dependence upon him. The Holy Spirit's job is to teach us the Word of God. Remember what Christ said: "But the Counselor, the Holy Spirit, whom the Father will send in my name, will teach you all things and will remind you of everything I have said to you" (John 14:26).

The Holy Spirit is the believer's resident professor. It is his job to teach the man of God the Word of God. In fact, we see David was aware of this principle as he prays for God to open his eyes so he could understand the law of God. Psalm 119:18 says, "Open my eyes that I may see wonderful things in your law."

David understood that in order to understand the Word of God—God's will—he needed grace. He needed the Spirit's illuminating work. It is entirely possible for a person to rely solely on his intellect and his research ability and not depend on the Holy Spirit.

42

However, James 4:6 says, "God opposes the proud but gives grace to the humble."

We must humble ourselves by coming to God in prayer and asking for his grace. That is how we learn God's will through his Word. We come to him dependently because we realize our incapability.

3. In order to be filled by God's will, we must be dependent upon mature believers.

This is a God–given resource to help each one of us know his Word. However, it is often neglected. Look at what Paul taught in Ephesians 4:11–13:

> *It was he who gave some to be apostles, some to be prophets, some to be evangelists, and some to be pastors and teachers,* to prepare God's people for works of service, so that the body of Christ may be built up *until we all reach unity in the faith and in the knowledge of the Son of God* and become mature, attaining to the whole measure of the fullness of Christ.

God gives pastors and teachers to help us reach a unity of the faith and the knowledge of the Son of God. Godly pastors and teachers are gifts to the church and we must take advantage of them. We do that by sitting under the local pastors and small group leaders God has given us and also through reading literature from gifted Bible teachers. Often God will use them to lead us into the knowledge of his will.

Some people will say that all we need is the Holy Spirit. Yes, that's true. But, the Holy Spirit commonly speaks through gifted teachers to help us better understand God's Word and his will for our life. That's essentially what Paul says in 1 Corinthians 12:21: "The eye cannot say to the hand, 'I don't need you!' And the head cannot say to the feet, 'I don't need you!'"

Yes, there is a dependence we should have upon one another. We should avail ourselves by asking questions and doing research because these mature believers have been given to us for that reason. If we ignore our relationship with mature believers, we may find that we lack the knowledge of God's will in our lives, which undoubtedly at some point will reap consequences on our lives or the lives of others.

4. In order to be filled by God's will, we must study the Word of God.

Certainly, there is no substitute for one's individual study of Scripture. We must work hard in studying the Word of God. Listen to what Paul said to Timothy: "Do your best to present yourself to God as one approved, a workman who does not need to be ashamed and who correctly handles the word of truth" (2 Tim. 2:15).

"Do your best" can be translated as "be diligent," and the KJV translates it as "study." How does a person receive the approval of God? He does his best; he is diligent in studying the Word of God so he can correctly handle it.

I think when we go before the judgment seat of Christ, many will not be approved (cf. 2 Cor. 5:10). They won't be approved because they weren't diligent. They didn't do their best. They didn't study to know God's will for their marriage, for their career, or for their children. For most Christians, the word "study" in conjunction with the Word of God isn't even in their vocabulary.

To read alone isn't to study. If you showed up for a test and all you did was listen to the lecture and read through the notes, you probably would not do well. To study means to wrestle with the Scripture, to ask it questions, to memorize it.

When most people see something in the Scripture that they don't understand, they just say, "Oh, God understands," or "My pastor probably understands." No, God has individually given you the Scripture and he wants you to understand it. It is important for your life. I talk to people all the time who say, "Oh, that doesn't really matter. All that matters is that we love." If that was all God wanted for you, he would have shortened the Bible by simply saying, "Love God with all your heart and love your neighbor as yourself." However, that's not the only thing in the Scripture.

In order to be filled with the knowledge of God's will, we must desire to know God's Word, which is where most of us fail. In addition, we must depend upon God and mature believers, and we must diligently study. There are no shortcuts to being filled with the knowledge of God's will. We should constantly pray for this.

5. To be filled with the knowledge of God's will, we must submit to God's Word.

As I mentioned before, to be "filled" means to be controlled by it (cf. Eph. 5:18). In order to be controlled by it, we must both have the knowledge and we must be willing to submit to it.

Listen to what Christ said about God's will: "Father, if you are willing, take this cup from me; yet not my will, but yours be done" (Luke 22:42).

Jesus willingly submitted to God's will even when it meant pain and suffering. Abraham willingly submitted to God's will even when it meant losing his son. Job willingly submitted to God's will even in the midst of the trial. He declared in Job 1:21: "Naked I came from my mother's womb, and naked I will depart. The LORD gave and the LORD has taken away; may the name of the LORD be praised."

Many Christians only want to submit to God's will when things are good or when things make sense to them. But true submission means submitting even when we don't understand or when it conflicts with our desires.

So many Christians find themselves angry with God when things don't go their way or when he allows trials to happen in their lives. They shake their fist at God. True submission to God's will means yielding under the sovereign hand of God in the midst of our trials (cf. 1 Peter 5:6).

An Avenue to Know God's Will

Let it also be known that submission to God's will is also the avenue to knowing God's will. Many Christians are praying for what's next or for what God wants them to do. Sometimes God doesn't reveal those things because even if he revealed it, we wouldn't choose to go that path.

A submissive heart is the secret to revelation—a secret to knowing his will. Let me show you a verse that teaches this reality. John 7:17 says, "If anyone chooses to do God's will, he will find out whether my teaching comes from God or whether I speak on my own."

Jesus, in speaking to all the onlookers, said if you want to know if I am the messiah, if you want to know if I am the only way to God, if you want to know that I was from the beginning of time, you must want to do God's will.

If you want to do God's will, then he will let you know if it's true. This is the reason so many people get stuck in doctrinal strongholds. They were raised in a certain teaching, or they think a certain teaching is right, because of their denomination or culture, and ultimately they really don't want to do God's will. They only want to support what they already believe. Therefore, they don't have the submissive heart needed to truly discern what is true or false. Knowledge comes from wanting to do God's will.

As Paul prayed this for the Colossian church, we must pray this for one another. "Lord, help our sister to know your will as she is looking at her future. Let her be filled with your knowledge on a daily basis at work. Lord, don't let her just know what your will says, but give her grace to submit to it." This is God's will for the church.

Identification of Believers

The church should be identified as people who are consumed with the will of God. They pray for it; they seek it; they study it; they practice it. Look at what

Christ said about his disciples: "To the Jews who had believed him, Jesus said, 'If you hold to my teaching, you are really my disciples'" (John 8:31).

True believers hold to Christ's teaching. They hold on to God's will. When Christ spoke of turning false professors away from him in the end times, it was because they were not consumed with God's will as all true believers are. Look what he said: "Not everyone who says to me, 'Lord, Lord,' will enter the kingdom of heaven, but only he who does the will of my Father who is in heaven" (Matt. 7:21).

These are the only ones who are truly saved: the ones who do the will of God. True believers are consumed with it and it is demonstrated in their prayers. This is how the Spirit of God leads believers to pray.

Reflection

1. What steps to knowing God's will stood out to you most and why?
2. How is God calling you to seek to know his will more through his Word?
3. What other questions or thoughts do you have about this section?
4. In what ways can you pray in response? Take a second to pray as the Lord leads.

Spirit–led Prayer Seeks the Benefits of Knowing and Doing God's Will

"And we pray this in order that you may live a life worthy of the Lord and may please him in every way: bearing fruit in every good work, growing in the knowledge of God" (Col. 1:10).

What results will you see in a congregation that is being filled with the knowledge of God's will? When Paul uses the phrase "in order," he is giving us a result clause. He is telling us why we pray for people to be filled with the knowledge of God's will. He is giving the benefits of knowing and doing God's will.

As we look at these benefits, it should also tell us if we are being filled with God's will. If we are being filled with God's will, these benefits will be in our lives. If not, then certainly this must not only be our prayer for others, but it also must be our endeavor and prayer for ourselves. Are we being filled with the knowledge of God's will, and can we see the fruits of this knowledge?

What are the results of being filled with the knowledge of God's will?

Worthy Walk

"And we pray this in order that you may live a *life worthy of the Lord*" (Col. 1:10).

A result of being filled with the knowledge of God's will is that believers will walk "worthy of the Lord." The word "worthy" comes from the root word "worth," how much something costs or should be valued. When Christians walk "worthy" of the Lord, they demonstrate the Lord's incredible worth in their lives. Their lives show how much God really means to them.

Sadly, the lives of many Christians do not demonstrate how meaningful God is to them. Their relationship with the Lord doesn't change their language; it doesn't change how they respond when people hurt them or when a job situation is unpleasant. Paul realizes that a full understanding of the Word of God—God's will—changes the way a person lives.

Please God in Every Way

"And we pray this in order that you may live a life worthy of the Lord and *may please him in every way*" (Col. 1:10).

Paul also says that knowledge of God's will, will enable the believer to please God in every way. This is very significant. I think we get a good picture of this when we study the book of Kings.

There was a common phrase used for the kings who pleased God. It would say, "they walked in the ways of David" (cf. 2 Kings 22:2). God was so pleased with David that he compared other kings to him. The evil kings were compared to Jeroboam of the northern kingdom, who set up a false worship system (cf. 2 Kings 13:2).

Some kings fully pleased God; some did not please him at all, and others were compromisers. The compromisers were those who followed the ways of David except in that they kept the high places. Listen to what Scripture said about Solomon: "Solomon showed his love for the LORD by walking according to the statutes of his father David, except that he offered sacrifices and burned incense on the high places" (1 Kings 3:3).

King Solomon was just like his father, except that he kept the high places. God had called for Israel to not worship like the pagan nations. Pagans often had high places where they sacrificed children and cried out to other gods. The God of Israel had called the nation to worship at the tabernacle, and later the temple, and gave them specific requirements about what worship should look like.

King Solomon pleased God, except for worshipping at the high places. This was true of many kings. Many kings truly loved God but were compromisers. Their lives displeased God because they looked just like the world.

In the same way, many Christians love God and follow God like David but have areas in their lives off-limits to God. It may be their entertainment (what they watch, listen to, or the way they get it), or it may be cheating on tests or taxes. It may be saying curse words here or there. They try to follow God in every other way except for a few high places where they are just like the world.

Many churches are like this as well. Overall, they are good, but in a few ways they displease God. If they don't repent, God will ultimately judge them (cf. Revelation Chapters 2 and 3). See, God doesn't want any of our ways to displease him. He desires us to be filled with the Word of God and controlled by it. He desires a life that seeks to please him in every way.

Let us pray that our church and our lives would please him in every way. Let us get rid of everything that is not acceptable to God.

Bearing Fruit in Every Good Work

"And we pray this in order that you may live a life worthy of the Lord and may please him in every way: *bearing fruit in every good work*, growing in the knowledge of God" (Col. 1:10).

The next benefit of a life that is filled with the will of God is bearing fruit in every good work. *What does it mean to bear fruit? What are some examples of fruit that should be in the life of a believer?*

- Fruit includes winning souls to Christ.

Look at how Paul spoke about the house of Stephanas. First Corinthians 16:15 says, "You know that the household of Stephanas were the first converts in Achaia, and they have devoted themselves to the service of the saints."

The phrase "first converts" is translated "firstfruits" in the KJV. Leading people to Christ is a fruit that comes from being filled with the Word of God.

- Fruit includes praise and worship to God.

"Through Jesus, therefore, let us continually offer to God *a sacrifice of praise—the fruit of lips* that confess his name" (Heb. 13:15).

Worshiping God and giving thanks in all situations instead of complaining and arguing is a fruit of being filled with the Word of God.

- Fruit includes giving to build the kingdom of God.

Paul talked about the churches giving money to the suffering church in Jerusalem as fruit. Look at Romans 15:26, 28:

For Macedonia and Achaia were pleased to make a contribution for the poor among the saints in Jerusalem. . . . So after I have completed this task and *have made sure that they have received this fruit*, I will go to Spain and visit you on the way.

- Fruit includes the inner heart attitudes.

We see this in the fruit of the Spirit in Galatians 5:22–23. "But the fruit of the Spirit is love, joy, peace, patience, kindness, goodness, faithfulness, gentleness and self–control. Against such things there is no law."

- Fruit includes acts of righteousness.

The writer of Hebrews talks about righteousness as fruit in the life of a believer. Hebrews 12:11 says, "No discipline seems pleasant at the time, but painful. Later on, however, it produces a harvest of righteousness and peace for those who have been trained by it." Harvest of righteousness can also be translated "fruits of righteousness" as in the KJV.

What's another result of being filled with his will?

Increasing in the Knowledge of God

"And we pray this in order that you may live a life worthy of the Lord and may please him in every way: bearing fruit in every good work, *growing in the knowledge of God*" (Col. 1:10).

One of the benefits of being filled with the knowledge of God's will is that it enables us to increase in the knowledge of God or get to know God better. It's very interesting that Paul includes this after bearing the fruits of righteousness.

This is true because when a person bears fruit, God will give him more of himself. We see this taught by Christ in Mark 4:24–25. Look at what he says:

> 'Consider carefully what you hear,' he continued. *'With the measure you use, it will be measured to you—and even more. Whoever has will be given more; whoever does not have, even what he has will be taken from him.'*

When a person uses the Word God has taught him and bears fruit, God blesses him by giving him more. God gives more understanding of the Word of God; he gives more intimacy with him. "Whoever has will be given more." This is a promise to those who obey God's will and don't simply listen to it every Sunday. James 1:25 says the same thing: "But the man who looks intently into the perfect law that gives freedom, and continues to do this, not forgetting what he has heard, but doing it—he will be blessed in what he does."

The person who looks at the Word of God and does what it says will be blessed by God. He receives more of who God is. But the person who is just a hearer and not a doer starts to have what he has learned taken away.

It has often been said that the reason nothing can live in the Dead Sea is because there is "inflow" but no "outflow." When a fish swims into the Dead Sea, it automatically dies.

Many Christians always hear but never do what the Word of God says. They never bear fruit, and, therefore, instead of growing and increasing in the knowledge of God, to them God feels farther away than before.

One of the reasons we should pray in accordance with the Spirit is for the benefit of "increasing in the knowledge of God" and growing in intimacy with him.

Spiritual Power Demonstrated in Moral Excellence

"*Being strengthened with all power* according to his glorious might so that you may have great *endurance and patience, and joyfully giving thanks to the Father,* who has qualified you to share in the inheritance of the saints in the kingdom of light" (Col. 1:11–12).

The final benefit of being filled with the knowledge of God's will is growing in the power of God. One might think that this power would be used for healings, prophecy, resurrections from the dead, or some other charismatic work, but it's not. A person who is filled with the knowledge of God's will has all power to endure, to be patient, to be joyful, and to give thanks.

Scripture would say that these are actually greater works than many miracles. When David controlled his anger while being mocked by Shimei, that was a greater victory than the miracle of defeating Goliath (2 Sam. 16:5–13). Listen to what Solomon said: "Better a patient man than a warrior, a man who controls his temper than one who takes a city" (Prov. 16:32).

Scripture says to control or rule one's own temper is greater than any military victory. As a result of Paul's prayer, God would give power to these believers to grow in these characteristics. Let's look a little closer at them.

Endurance

Endurance means to bear up under a heavy weight. Through prayer God gives us power to endure a tough work situation, a difficult relationship, or a trial. This power comes through prayer.

It is often said you are either in a trial or about to enter one. Christianity does not exempt a person from the trials of life; it actually may cause more trials.

However, God gives us the precious fruit of the Spirit to endure.

Patience

It has been said that the difference between patience and endurance is that patience primarily has to do with people. God gives us power to *endure hard situations without complaining or giving up,* and he gives us power to *endure difficult people without retaliation.*

Joy

Joy is an inward attitude that has nothing to do with circumstances but is based on one's relationship with God. A person controlled by the will of God can go through a difficult situation with joy. Paul said this: *"Sorrowful, yet always rejoicing*; poor, yet making many rich; having nothing, and yet possessing everything" (2 Cor. 6:10).

God can give power to have joy, even in the midst of suffering. Let that be our prayer.

Thanksgiving

Thanksgiving has to do with the outward expression of this internal joy in all circumstances. We saw this perfectly modeled by Job as he thanked God even in the midst of his trials. This was a man "filled with the knowledge of God's will." Listen again to what he said: "Naked I came from my mother's womb, and naked I will depart. The LORD gave and the

LORD has taken away; may the name of the LORD be praised" (Job 1:21).

For many Christians, we are not only guilty of not giving God thanks or praise when things are bad, but we often forget to give thanks when things are good or when God answers our prayers. We saw this with the ten lepers who approached Christ in Luke 17. He told them to go to the temple and show themselves to the priest. On the way there, all of them were healed. One of them was so happy and grateful he ran back to tell Christ, "Thank you." Consider how Jesus responded: "Were not all ten cleansed? Where are the other nine? Was no one found to return and give praise to God except this foreigner?" (Luke 17:17–18).

Everybody went their own way and only one returned to give God thanks. Giving thanks to God in trial and in blessing is a result of being filled with the knowledge of God's will. We should pray for this.

It seems the primary avenue of thanksgiving that remains in the life of a person who is being filled with the knowledge of God's will is *thankfulness for his or her salvation*. That seems to be what Paul is referring to when he says "with thanksgiving." Look at what he says:

> *Giving thanks to the Father, who has qualified you to share in the inheritance of the saints in the kingdom of light.* For he has rescued us from the dominion of darkness and brought us into the kingdom of the Son he loves, in whom we have redemption, the forgiveness of sins (Col. 1:12–14).

A never-ending thanksgiving for salvation should be happening in the life of a believer. Sadly, for many of us, including myself, we often lose thanksgiving for the greatest thing that happened in our lives—our salvation. This should be a constant source of joy even in suffering.

David prayed this: "Restore to me the joy of your salvation and grant me a willing spirit, to sustain me" (Ps. 51:12). Thanksgiving should be a constant in the believer's life. "Give thanks in all circumstances for this is God's will for you in Christ Jesus" (1 Thess. 5:18).

Have you lost the joy of your salvation?

When a person fails a test on the same day he won a million dollar lottery, do you think he would still be walking around discouraged and depressed? Absolutely not! Why? It's because his success is so much greater than his loss. He could take care of his future if he is wise with that money. Saint, your future has already been taken care of. God has qualified you to be part of the kingdom of his Son. He has delivered you from darkness into the kingdom of light.

A person who is filled with the knowledge of God's will, will never forget this. It's constantly inside of them—on their heart and mind. Let's look at how Peter comforts a church being persecuted for the faith in 1 Peter. They had lost land, family members, jobs, and their dignity for Christ. How do you think he would start a letter to people in such an unfortunate situation? Watch.

> *Praise be to the God and Father of our Lord Jesus Christ*! In his great mercy he has *given us new birth* into a living hope through the

resurrection of Jesus Christ from the dead, and into an *inheritance that can never perish, spoil or fade—kept in heaven for you* (1 Peter 1:3–4).

Praise God for his great mercy in saving us! Praise God that even though we lost our inheritance on earth, we have an inheritance that can never perish, spoil or fade—kept in heaven for us! Many of us have lost this. It is God's will for us to always give thanks and to never lose thanksgiving for the greatest event that ever happened in our lives—our salvation.

The benefits of being filled with the knowledge of God's will are walking worthy of him, pleasing him in every way, bearing fruits for the kingdom, having power that enables us to endure, be patient, joyful, and thankful. We should pray for these characteristics in our lives and the lives of other believers.

Are you filled with the knowledge of God's will? And are you seeing these wonderful benefits in your life?

Reflection

1. Which one of these characteristics of being filled with God's will were most challenging to you and why?
2. How is God calling you to pursue spiritual growth in these characteristics?
3. What other questions or thoughts do you have about this section?
4. In what ways can you pray in response? Take a second to pray as the Lord leads.

Conclusion

When we look at Paul in this passage, we learn something about Spirit–led prayer. His prayer was so in tune with the Spirit of God that God chose to place it in the Holy Scripture so we can learn from it and put it into practice in our prayer life.

What are characteristics of Spirit–led prayer?

1. Spirit–led prayer is informed.
2. Spirit–led prayer is constant.
3. Spirit–led prayer asks for God–sized requests.
4. Spirit–led Prayer is consumed with God's will.
5. Spirit–led prayer seeks the benefits of knowing and doing God's will.

In what ways is God challenging you to grow in your prayer life? For whom and for what is God calling you to pray?

Walking the Romans Road

How can a person be saved? From what is he saved? How can someone have eternal life? Scripture teaches that after death each person will spend eternity either in heaven or hell. How can a person go to heaven?

Paul said this to Timothy:

> But as for you, continue in what you have learned and have become convinced of, because you know those from whom you learned it, and how from infancy you have known the holy Scriptures, which are *able to make you wise for salvation through faith in Christ Jesus.*
> 2 Timothy 3:14-15

One of the reasons God gave us Scripture is to make us wise for salvation. This means that without it nobody can know how to be saved.

Well then, how can a people be saved and what are they being saved from? A common method of sharing the good news of salvation is through the Romans Road. One of the great themes, not only of the Bible, but specifically of the book of Romans is salvation. In Romans, the author, Paul, clearly details the steps we must take in order to be saved.

How can we be saved? What steps must we take?

Step One: We Must Accept that We Are Sinners

Romans 3:23 says, "For all have sinned and fall short of the glory of God." What does it mean to sin? The word sin means "to miss the mark." The mark we missed is looking like God. When God created mankind in the Genesis narrative, he created man in the "image of God" (1:27). The "image of God" means many things, but probably, most importantly it means we were made to be holy just as he is holy. Man was made moral. We were meant to reflect God's holiness in every way: the way we think, the way we talk, and the way we act. And any time we miss the mark in these areas, we commit sin.

Furthermore, we do not only sin when we commit a sinful act such as: lying, stealing, or cheating; again, we sin anytime we have a wrong heart motive. The greatest commandments in Scripture are to "Love God with all our heart, mind, and soul and to love others as ourselves" (Matt 22:36-40, paraphrase). Whenever we don't love God supremely and love others as ourselves, we sin and fall short of the glory of God. For this reason, man is always in a state of sinning. Sadly, even if our actions are good, our heart is bad. I have never loved God with my whole heart, mind, and soul and neither has anybody else. Therefore, we have all sinned and fall short of the glory of God (Rom 3:23). We have all missed the mark of God's holiness and we must accept this.

What's the next step?

Step Two: We Must Understand We Are under the Judgment of God

Why are we under the judgment of God? It is because of our sins. Scripture teaches God is not only a loving God, but he is a just God. And his justice requires judgment for each of our sins. Romans 6:23 says, "For the wages of sin is death."

A wage is something we earn. Every time we sin, we earn the wage of death. What is death? Death really means separation. In physical death, the body is separated from the spirit, but in spiritual death, man is separated from God. Man currently lives in a state of spiritual death (cf. Eph 2:1-3). We do not love God, obey him, or know him as we should. Therefore, man is in a state of death.

Moreover, one day at our physical death, if we have not been saved, we will spend eternity separated from God in a very real hell. In hell, we will pay the wage for each of our sins. Therefore, in hell people will experience various degrees of punishment (cf. Lk 12:47-48). This places man in a very dangerous predicament—unholy and therefore under the judgment of God.

How should we respond to this? This leads us to our third step.

Step Three: We Must Recognize God Has Invited All to Accept His Free Gift of Salvation

Romans 6:23 does not stop at the wages of sin being death. It says, "For the wages of sin is death, but the gift of God is eternal life through Jesus Christ our Lord." Because God loved everybody on the earth, he offered the free gift of eternal life, which anyone can receive through Jesus Christ.

Because it is a gift, it cannot be earned. We cannot work for it. Ephesians 2:8-9 says, "For it is by grace you have been saved, through faith—and this not from yourselves, it is the gift of God—not by works, so that no one can boast."

Going to church, being baptized, giving to the poor, or doing any other righteous work does not save. Salvation is a gift that must be received from God. It is a gift that has been prepared by his effort alone.

How do we receive this free gift?

Step Four: We Must Believe Jesus Christ Died for Our Sins and Rose from the Dead

If we are going to receive this free gift, we must believe in God's Son, Jesus Christ. Because God loved us, cared for us, and didn't want us to be separated from him eternally, he sent his Son to die for our sins. Romans 5:8 says, "But God demonstrates his own love for us in this: While we were still sinners, Christ died for us." Similarly, John 3:16 says, "For God so loved the world that he gave his only begotten son that whosoever believeth in him should not perish but have eternal life." God so loved us that he gave his only Son for our sins.

Jesus Christ was a real, historical person who lived 2,000 years ago. He was born of a virgin. He lived a perfect life. He was put to death by the Romans and the Jews. And he rose again on the third day. In his death, he took our sins and God's wrath for them and gave us his perfect righteousness so we could be accepted by God. Second Corinthians 5:21 says, "God made him who had no sin to be sin for us, so that in him we might become the righteousness of God." God did all this so we could be saved from his wrath.

Christ's death satisfied the just anger of God over our sins. When God saw Jesus on the cross, he saw us and our sins and therefore judged Jesus. And now, when God sees those who are saved, he sees his righteous Son and accepts us. In salvation, we have become the righteousness of God.

If we are going to be saved, if we are going to receive this free gift of salvation, we must believe in Christ's death, burial, and resurrection for our sins (cf. 1 Cor 15:3-5, Rom 10:9-10). Do you believe?

Step Five: We Must Confess Christ as Lord of Our Lives

Romans 10:9-10 says,

> That if you confess with your mouth, "Jesus is Lord," and believe in your heart that God raised him from the dead, you will be saved. For it is with your heart that you believe and are justified, and it is with your mouth that you confess and are saved.

Not only must we believe, but we must confess Christ as Lord of our lives. It is one thing to believe in Christ but another thing to follow Christ. Simple belief does not save. Christ must be our Lord. James said this: "Even the demons believe and shudder" (James 2:19) but the demons are not saved—Christ is not their Lord.

Another aspect of making Christ Lord is *repentance*. Repentance really means a change of mind that leads to a change of direction. Before we met Christ, we were living our own life and following our own sinful desires. But when we get saved, our mind and direction change. We start to follow Christ as Lord.

How do we make this commitment to the lordship of Christ so we can be saved? Paul said we must confess with our mouth "Jesus is Lord" as we believe in him. Romans 10:13 says, "Everyone who calls on the name of the Lord will be saved."

If you admit that you are a sinner and understand you are under God's wrath because of them; if you believe Jesus Christ is the Son of God, that he died on the cross for your sins, and rose from the dead for your salvation; if you are ready to turn from your sin and cling to Christ as Lord, you can be saved.

If this is your heart, then you can pray this prayer and commit to following Christ as your Lord.

> *Dear heavenly Father, I confess I am a sinner and have fallen short of your glory, what you made me for. I believe Jesus Christ died on the cross to pay the penalty for my sins and rose from the dead so I can have eternal life. I am turning away from my sin and accepting you as my Lord and Savior. Come into my life and change me. Thank you for your gift of salvation.*

Scripture teaches that if you truly accepted Christ as your Lord, then you are a new creation. Second Corinthians 5:17 says, "Therefore, if anyone is in Christ, he is a new creation; the old has gone, the new has come!" God has forgiven your sins (1 John

1:9), he has given you his Holy Spirit (Rom 8:15), and he is going to disciple you and make you into the image of his Son (cf. Rom 8:29). He will never leave you nor forsake you (Heb 13:5), and he will complete the work he has begun in your life (Phil 1:6). In heaven, angels and saints are rejoicing because of your commitment to Christ (Lk 15:7).

Praise God for his great salvation! May God keep you in his hand, empower you through the Holy Spirit, train you through mature believers, and use you to build his kingdom! "The one who calls you is faithful, he will do it" (1 Thess 5:24). God bless you!

Coming Soon

Praise the Lord for your interest in studying and teaching God's Word. If God has blessed you through the BTG series, please partner with us in petitioning God to greatly use this series to encourage and build his Church. Also, please consider leaving an Amazon review. By doing this, you help spread the "Word." Thanks for your partnership in the gospel from the first day until now (Phil 1:4-5).

Available:
First Peter
Nehemiah
Colossians
Theology Proper
Building Foundations for a Godly Marriage
God's Battle Plan for Purity
Characteristics of a Godly Marriage
Characteristics of Spirit-led Prayer

Coming Soon:
Philippians
Abraham
Ephesians

About the Author

Greg Brown earned his MA in religion and MA in teaching from Trinity International University, an MRE from Liberty University, and a PhD in theology from Louisiana Baptist University. He has served over ten years in pastoral ministry and currently serves as Chaplain and Assistant Professor at Handong Global University, pastor at Handong International Congregation, and as a Navy Reserve chaplain.

Greg married his lovely wife Tara Jayne in 2006, and they have one daughter, Saiyah Grace. He enjoys going on dates with his wife, playing with his daughter, reading, writing, studying in coffee shops, working out, and following the NBA and UFC. His pursuit in life, simply stated, is "to know God and to be found faithful by Him."

To connect with Greg, please follow at http://www.pgregbrown.com.

Notes

[i] J. F. MacArthur Jr., *MacArthur New Testament Commentary: Colossians.* (Chicago: Moody Press, 1992), 25.
[ii] Teacher's Outline and Study Bible – Commentary – Teacher's Outline and Study Bible – Colossians: The Teacher's Outline and Study Bible.
[iii] Lorne C. Sanny, *The Pathfinder: A Condensed Life Story of Dawson E. Trotman*

Notes